Exploring Citizenship

Acting Responsibly

Vic Parker

Heinemann Library,
Chicago, IL

www.heinemannraintree.com

Visit our website to find out more information about Heinemann-Raintree books.

To order:

☎ Phone 888-454-2279

🖥 Visit www.heinemannraintree.com to browse our catalog and order online.

Edited by Rebecca Rissman and Catherine Veitch
Designed by Ryan Frieson and Betsy Wernert
Picture research by Elizabeth Alexander and Rebecca Sodergren
Production by Duncan Gilbert
Originated by Heinemann Library
Printed in China by South China Printing Company Ltd

Library of Congress Cataloging-in-Publication Data
Parker, Victoria.
  Acting responsibly / Vic Parker. -- 1st ed.
    p. cm. -- (Exploring citizenship)
  Includes bibliographical references and index.
  ISBN 978-1-4329-3315-9 (hc) -- ISBN 978-1-4329-3323-4 (pb) 1.
Responsibility. [1. Conduct of life.] I. Title.
BJ1451.P37 2008
179'.9--dc22
                          2008055305

Acknowledgments

We would like to thank the following for permission to reproduce photographs: Alamy **pp. 7** (© John Eccles), **9** (© Jupiterimages/Polka Dot), **13** (© Andersen Ross/Blend Images), **22** (© Urban Zone), **24** (© Blickwinkel/Hecker), **28** (© Design Pics Inc); Corbis **pp. 6** (© Paul Barton), **8** (© Fancy/Veer), **10** (© Judith Haeusler/Zefa), **14** (© Kevin Dodge), **15** (© Simon Marcus), **17** (© Fancy/Veer), **18** (© Fancy/Veer), **21** (© Roy Botterell); Getty Images **p. 12** (Kate Powers/Taxi); iStockphoto **pp. 23, 25** (© Mark Stokes); Photolibrary **pp. 4** (SW Productions/Brand X Pictures), **5** (Frank Siteman/AGE Fotostock), **16** (Marc Debnam/Digital Vision), **19** (Phoebe Dunn), **26** (Corbis), **27** (Stephen Shepherd/Garden Picture Library); Shutterstock **p. 29** (© Monkey Business Images).

Cover photograph of a girl with a dog reproduced with permission of Shutterstock (© Sonya Etchison).

The publishers would like to thank Yael Biederman for her help in the preparation of this book.

Every effort has been made to contact copyright holders of any material reproduced in this book. Any omissions will be rectified in subsequent printings if notice is given to the publisher.

Contents

Some words are shown in bold, **like this**. You can find out what they mean by looking in the glossary.

What Is Citizenship?

Citizenship is about being a member of a group such as a family, a school, or a country. A citizen has **rights** and **responsibilities**. Having rights means there are certain ways that other people should treat you.

Working together in a group can be lots of fun.

When you behave thoughtfully, people want to spend time with you.

To be a good citizen you need to think about how your behavior affects your life and the lives of other people. If you behave thoughtfully, carefully, and kindly, your life and other people's lives will be happier and easier. This is called acting responsibly.

What Are Responsibilities?

If you have pets, you are responsible for taking care of them.

A **responsibility** is a **duty** to do something, such as to remember to feed your dog or clean your room. However, a responsibility can also be a duty not to do something, such as *not* turning on the television when you have homework or chores to do.

You are responsible for your own safety when you ride a bicycle.

Being responsible makes you feel good about yourself. It also makes others **respect** and appreciate you. Adults will give you more freedom to do things on your own if you act responsibly.

Responsibility for Our Bodies

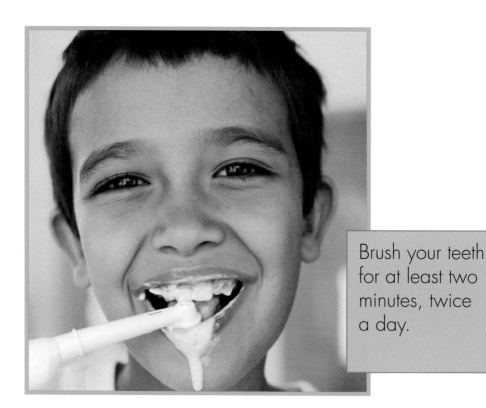

Brush your teeth for at least two minutes, twice a day.

You need to take care of your body to stay healthy. Every day, you have the **responsibility** to wash yourself, comb your hair, and brush your teeth. You are also responsible for eating well and getting enough sleep.

When you wash your hands, you are helping yourself and other people to stay healthy.

If you do not keep yourself clean, you might spread germs that could make you or other people sick. It is responsible to cover your nose and mouth when you cough or sneeze. It is also very important to wash your hands after you have used the bathroom.

9

Responsibilities at Home

At home, there are always lots of chores to do, such as setting the table, making your bed, and cleaning up. Being responsible means helping to do these chores.

Helping at home can make you feel good.

Here are some chores at home that you can take responsibility for doing:

☑ keeping your bedroom neat
☑ helping to clean the house
☑ helping to wash the car
☑ helping in the yard
☑ washing or drying dishes
☑ putting clean dishes away.

Can you think of any more?

Think about it

How would you feel if you were the only person in your home doing any chores?

School Responsibilities

At school, there are lots of ways you can act responsibly. You can listen carefully to your teacher and answer politely. You can look for ways to help your teacher and your classmates. You can also be kind to everyone you meet during the school day.

In all your classes there are jobs you can do to help the coach or teacher.

If you try hard, people will want to help you.

Being responsible also means remembering to do your homework the best you can. It is a good idea to try hard with all your school **responsibilities**, because this will help you to do well when you are older.

13

Responsibilities in Our Free Time

When people think of others, everybody has more fun.

When you are in a playground, you can act responsibly by thinking about the people around you. You should take turns and also look out for younger children who might need help. Try not to rush or bump into other people.

Make sure you always put trash in the right place.

You should try to be careful with the playground **equipment** so it does not break. You should also keep everything clean and neat. This way, other people can have fun using the playground, just like you.

15

Being Responsible for Possessions

Everybody has special belongings, such as toys, books, and pocket money. You can act responsibly by being careful with these things and making sure they do not get damaged or lost.

When you put away your things, you will not lose any small pieces.

Always be careful with library books you borrow, so they can be used by other people.

You should **respect** things that belong to other people by treating them as if they were your own things. If you are allowed to borrow things for a while, you should make sure they do not get damaged. You should also return them on time.

Getting Ready to Go Out

It is helpful to think ahead when you get ready to go out.

It is your **responsibility** to get to school on time each day and to have everything you need with you. It is a good idea to get your bag ready the night before. In the morning, make sure you get up in plenty of time.

It is also important to be ready for other activities, such as a music lesson or soccer practice. If you are late or forget your **equipment**, you may cause problems for your teacher, coach, or teammates. Being late or forgetting equipment is not acting responsibly.

Make sure you are ready before an activity starts so other people do not have to wait for you.

Acting Responsibly

You should always try to act responsibly when you are outside in order to keep both yourself and other people safe. Here are some things you can do:

- ☑ Never jump off the sidewalk into the street.
- ☑ Never play ball games on the sidewalk.
- ☑ Never wear headphones while walking along the sidewalk.
- ☑ Always cross the street at a safe, official crosswalk.
- ☑ Never cross the street without listening for traffic and looking each way several times.
- ☑ When you are crossing the street, always remember to look out for bicycles and motorcycles as well as cars, trucks, and buses.

Whenever you are outside, you can act responsibly by thinking about the people around you. If you come face to face with people who are old, people in wheelchairs, or people with strollers, you can move aside to let them go past instead of making them go around you.

Carry skateboards until you find a safe place to skate.

Taking Responsibility for Your Safety

You may sometimes see signs that say: *Do Not Touch!*, *Keep Out!*, or *Private!* It is important that you **respect** these signs and do what they say. This is because they are often important **instructions** to keep us safe from danger.

Always read safety signs when you are in a new place.

You are acting responsibly when you do not touch the things in the list below. This is because they are difficult to use without an adult's help and might hurt you.

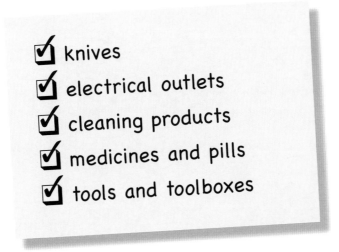

- ☑ knives
- ☑ electrical outlets
- ☑ cleaning products
- ☑ medicines and pills
- ☑ tools and toolboxes

Can you think of any more?

Many household products could harm you.

Acting Responsibly in the Countryside

You can look at wildlife, but do not touch it.

The countryside is a beautiful place, but it would not stay that way if everybody trampled through fields and picked all the flowers. You can act responsibly in the countryside by sticking to paths whenever you can and leaving wild things where you find them.

Leave nature just as you found it.

You can take **responsibility** for caring for wild animals, too. Do not leave litter that might harm creatures. For instance, a plastic bag might get caught over an animal's or bird's head and stop it from breathing. Always remember to shut gates behind you so farm animals do not get out of their fields.

25

Taking Responsibility for the Environment

We should all act responsibly to take care of the **environment**. A very important thing you can do is to **recycle** your garbage instead of throwing it away. This means that there is less waste to be buried in big **landfill sites**, which take up lots of space in the ground.

Remember to recycle your paper, glass, metal, plastic, and clothes.

RECYCLE

Saving water is acting responsibly.

You can collect rainwater in a **rain barrel** to water plants. You can turn off televisions, DVD players, computers, and light bulbs to save electricity. There are many other ways to act responsibly for the environment.

The Importance of Acting Responsibly

It is important to act responsibly so that people will **trust** you. If people trust you, they will give you more freedom to do things on your own. This will make you feel good about yourself.

Acting responsibly will bring you closer to other people.

Acting responsibly checklist

☑ Think about how your actions will affect others.

☑ Remember when you should or should not do something.

☑ **Respect** other people and their property.

☑ Take care of our **environment**.

☑ Follow rules, such as those for safety.

Acting responsibly means that you will do well and stay safe and happy. Your life will be more enjoyable, and so will the lives of others.

Good friends respect each other.

Glossary

duty something that you have to do because it is your job or because you feel it is the right thing to do

environment land, water, and air in which people, animals, and plants live

equipment tools and clothing you need to do a certain activity or task

instructions information and advice about how to do something or how to use something

landfill site place where garbage is buried underground

rain barrel large container for collecting rain, which can then be used for watering plants

recycle save something so that it can be used again

respect way of treating someone or something with kindness and politeness

responsibility something that it is your job to deal with

right basic rule of good behavior that people should show toward you, such as being fair, thoughtful, and safe. Everyone else has these rights, too.

trust believing that someone will do the right thing

Find Out More

Books

Loewen, Nancy. *Do I Have To?: Kids Talk About Responsibility.* Mankato, Minn.: Picture Window, 2003.

Loewen, Nancy. *We Live Here Too: Kids Talk About Good Citizenship.* Mankato, Minn.: Picture Window, 2005.

Mayer, Cassie. *Being Helpful.* Chicago: Heinemann Library, 2008.

Mayer, Cassie. *Being Responsible.* Chicago: Heinemann Library, 2008.

Small, Mary. *Being a Good Citizen: A Book About Citizenship.* Mankato, Minn.: Picture Window, 2006.

Website

www.hud.gov/kids

This government Website shows children what it means to be good citizens.

Index